THE JOURN

HOME

The Journey Home

SCOTT HUMPHREYS

Copyright © 2019 Scott Humphreys.

First published in the UK
By Strangford publications
Shropshire

Scott Humphreys asserts the moral right to be identified as
the author of this work.

All Rights reserved.
No part of this publication may be reproduced, sorted in a
retrieval system, or transmitted in any form or by any means,
electronic, mechanical, photocopying, recording or otherwise,
without the prior permission of the publisher, except in the
case of brief quotation embodied in
articles and reviews.

ISBN: 9781702067768

To

Amy and Luke,

My guiding lights:

Do not mourn too long that my time has come,

For it is only in my desire to evolve that I am

Temporarily free of your perception.

When there is love, there is a bond which

Exists beyond time and space and as certain

as you are aware of your own being,

we will know each other again.

CONTENTS

CONTENTS

ACKNOWLEDGMENTS

A special thank you to Maisie Olah for her innovative analysis, and to Maisydel Fenn for all her hard work, encouragement and creativity in bringing this work to publication.

The Roll of a Drum

It rolls and rolls into its own oblivion,
            The velocity of each turn takes me
Further into the bleak abyss

            I lie motionless but for the rattle of its cage,
And wonder if the bleakness of my destiny
            Is any darker than the drum that contains me

Like its musical cousin, I hear an impending rhythm,
Trance like in its speed, yet still, I do not know who put me here,
Even less, why it never stops

            And as I lie unconcerned for what awaits me,
I drift in and out of consciousness while I sleep
            In the silence of the world in which I dream

Sleep, sleep and sleep.
            With each opening of my eyes,
I wonder more and more
            What is real and what is illusion.

Reach for the Sun

A hollow tree of fading years
Through storms of an age since past
And times of old we can only dream
How can it be that your blossom still lasts

Beside you and beneath you we seem so small
And still we forget our time has only just begun
Shaded by the comfort of your grand expression
Joyous in the knowledge we have to still to reach the sun.

Another Realm, Another World

The fading light seems hard to ignore
When you think you see a sparkle,

An avenue you failed to explore,
Inviting you to question, perhaps
You had imagined something more

And even though these thoughts
Are well designed, there is a question,

An image of sweetness you cannot define,
Of possibilities and variations
Some way out in time

Potentials untold, a story from a different place
In God we trust, in faith of his eternal grace

Emblem of another realm,
Another world and history,
We may one day embrace

And what right has a soul who has travelled
This way, to soften such innocence

Diminish or sway, decry an
Untainted heart, the garden she
Traverses and in which I no longer play

The seeds of creation burst forth like flowers
Of light, lay waste all sorrows, and thoughts

Of a starless night, given only
To remind us of our calling,
Our belonging, and all that is right.

Meadows of Time

In time we roll and in time we fall -
And in each new place we are never the same.
In life's purpose, we dance to it's call -
Eager to glance at the meadow of another plane.

The Solitude of Change

It really doesn't matter if I had a life before,
Of solitude and progression,
Held back from expression by the things I would ignore

And it didn't make a difference that I had died inside,
Made aware of my limitations,
And restricted by a relentless tide

It really didn't matter that no one cared,
Or looked back to say goodbye,
Or acknowledge the connections that were impaired

All that mattered was in their eyes
I was still someone they could share,
A shadow of myself, a little something to compare

I had changed, and despite the similarities,
The person I once paraded
Was no longer there.

The Eyes of Three Fish

The eyes of three fish that sparkle and shimmer
Like the surface of the ocean they create a mirror
Attached with symmetrical lines and guarded minds
A dance of graceful mermaids, you are never in time

And in the moments, you catch the blue waters of their gaze
Imaginary thoughts invite you to wonder their elusive maze
With curious hope there is an emotion you aspire
Wishing their pattern held a place for your desire.

Impetus to Create

Way out in a distant realm,
There was a place I once called home.
Where laughter filled the air,
And the excitement of a new direction
Held back fear of the unknown

In the ignorance of innocence
I dreamed only of love,
And as the sun set low in time
With my mind, I could almost reach out
And touch the emerging stars above

Like a half-forgotten dream,
You heard a song vibrate in rhymes
That made the senses ignite, and with
Playful thoughts, the skies were dancing
With imagination far out of sight

A time, not for remembering
But the reality you would leave
To destiny and fate, of a life
Yet unknown, but the potential for
Experiences you wish to create.

Escape from Time

I had a quarrel with Time last November

And he's been looking for me at tea since next September.

He was dozing while I slept and he didn't expect,

That I would wake so soon and quickly defect.

I caught him out and he wasn't content,

And he knows quite rightly I took off without his consent.

He will be annoyed when he catches my tail,

Because he knows while he dozed, I was quick to bail,

We will make it up in the end, it's just a little something to Amuse,

Another game with time I couldn't refuse.

But on this occasion, it is suspected he will be a little affected,

Because he knows I got much further than he ever expected.

Unspoken Words

When you dream upon a star
You never thought would come true,
And it flickered with probability,
Giving you courage to see it through.

You imagined a life with a person
You had no reason to entice or distract,
A dream half wished for, half designed,
No understanding on how to react

Even the realization there was
Maybe no future or little room to grow,
Few places to hide, and nowhere
In the avenues of our world for it to go.

Now I watch with sadness,
As this imaginary light passes me by,
It seems hard to let you go,
To see it diminish, an illusion left to die

I throw a dice to determine a future,
Gamble away the experience
Potentials lost in time,
Dreams gone awry without further interference

As the crossroads of intention
Reveals her calling in another direction
I begin to wonder, was it a word
Unspoken that severed the connection.

The Face in the Picture

The face of beauty that hung on the wall,
    Of exquisite emotions and loves that would fall
        And in the wondrous moments I shared in her grief,
            With time, her pensive eyes became less of a
    Relief.

I dreamed of a place and a person I did not know,
    And with a belief that without her I would never grow
        And when she appeared in the image I had projected,
            Our lives became an illusion that neither of us
    Accepted.

She wasn't anything more than I instinctively knew, the
    Image of her inner beauty never quite came true. She
        Was wonderfully human as I was compelled to admire,
            Yet that wasn't the face in the picture I had
    Aspired.

Invitation to Love

What did I do,
> That made you change the way you looked into my eyes?
> No longer a kindred spirit, but a person I only saw in disguise.

I had barely
> Opened the chapters and revealed the oceans of my mind. A
> Mosaic soul not easily embraced, but where your love would
> Be returned in kind.

As complex
> As it might have appeared, it wasn't designed to frighten or
> Sway. Just a curious assortment of life experiences like the
> Ones we created today.

If you had
> Stepped a little closer into the world you were invited, you may
> Have seen some of the reasons of why my emotions became
> Ignited.

Yet outside,
> You patiently waited and to all my logic you appeared to be
> There, but your mind had already left, and I sensed that you
> No longer cared.

Little Light of Creation

For something bright and from afar,
I had wished upon an unknown star

Her little hand around my finger secure
Her eyes of an innocence, an angel so pure

Through all those moments I wanted to cry
I knew that without her, I would surely die

A kindred soul from a like-minded place
Little light of creation, my own to embrace

With a protective hand that would never let go
Through the ages I would watch her grow

And now as life subsides, no more a primary goal
She still shines a light at the heart of my soul.

My Beautiful Boy

The light sets on wonderful nights and magical days
Reminiscing the turns of life, acknowledging the old ways

That time when you thought the moment was a setting sun
With the hope of new horizons, you thought would never come

Yet, it was not that fate had alluded a wishing thought
Or a lesson, it seemed a hundred times you had been taught

Just an image, the scatterings of a person you didn't know
Projections of a greater self in time you would one day grow.

Visions in Time

Strange how desire has a way of making you forget who you are,
Something that caught you unaware, like you're in reach of a star

And knowing inside, that for all its glitter,
It will only take you so far

I hear a whisper, it's a joyous distraction,
The rhythm of your heart

Follow it with all you wish,
And we will hold firm your eternal place

Treasuring the seeds of your imaginings, the epicenter of grace
And for all your inspiration, it's not something you can replace

Just visions in time, desires of creation
You are eager to embrace.

Passing Moments

We dance   around   the stars
Without thought,
Without question,
As if the   stars dance   around us too.

And even   when we   lose ourselves
To our beliefs, they are nothing more
Than a passing moment
Of our day,   of our night,   of our dawn.

We may   not   see them,
We may not feel their presence,
But they still shine to show us where we are.
And they   are never too far   from our sight.

Indigo Child

What is this magnetism that blew in from the trees,
    That took my mind, a forest flower on a summer breeze.

A flame of nature that opened a hole in time and space,
    Radiant connections sent out like golden threaded lace.

And the forest stood still, a leafy window to another world,
    To remind me of dreams from another time still unfulfilled.

Then I noticed her, a companion, a connection by my side.
    A fallen star, a purveyor to rejuvenate a soul that has died

Suddenly the world has stopped, and your life is on pause
    An Indigo child set forth in preparation for a sacred course.

Guardian of the Night

I sense what you are and I sense what you see,
And for some of those reasons you may be afraid of me.
I have looked into your fate and seen into your dreams,
An image of yourself that is not what it seems.

I feel your emotion, and from me you will learn more,
A glance into another dimension at the end of all wars.
I know you will see in some direction, that reflects a pure light,
I am simply the guardian that holds back the night.

Sanctuary of a Dream

I have a desire to speak,
      To share my thoughts
And let you know of a place in my mind
      Where I dreamed a magical realm,
Of equals in love and the expression of innocence defined

And while the distance is reflected
      And made real by the impending rise of another sun
The new dawn casts a shadow on this person
      I had dreamed
And hoped
      I would one day become

Yet time and her spontaneous ways
      Has finally caught up
And revealed her intention-
      To carry my sadness
To her sanctuary
      And lay down another fairytale
Of my invention.

Pray

To look upon the landscape of far off fields
A wish cast out, in mind her dancing yields
To seek out the magical places she conceals.

I often thought about the future that way

But now it's just a place I had seen and dreamed
Barely the shadow of a world it once seemed
The directions I hoped my life would be redeemed.

I have often thought the past was not for play

Now as I review time in so many different ways
And all my aspirations and the desires she raised
Towards unknown worlds, these thoughts I gazed.

I have often thought, is this why I no longer pray.

A Patch of Garden

There is a place in my garden without any flowers
          A patch I had hoped would possess some otherworldly powers
              Whilst I looked down on an oasis of things I desired,
      To share with a person, to be made real and inspired

And the times I thought I had planted something real
              It never seemed to manifest any love that I could feel
                  Now as I see it die, and become an illusion in space
      I am reminded of the lost worlds I failed to embrace

A temple set aside, a sanctuary for my imagination
              Fairytales of my mind that often lead me to temptation
                  And the times I hoped to find it come alive with creation
      It only ever flickered a fading light of a different sensation.

Message to the Unknown

What is this intriguing flower
That flutters and deflects,
Where even logic has little
Understanding of its enticing effects

Like a shadow in the rain
That dampens the flames in your mind
Unsure of where it is taking you,
Another world of a different kind

Can this really be why I
Am so drawn to this perfection,
And yet still unsure of her song,
And how she sings in an uncertain direction

This is not a place I envisioned,
Or a choice I want to ponder,
When there are too many places
In the forest of her mind I am left to wonder

Mirror of Distraction

So, the dream has ended and the union I imagined
    Left no lasting impression. The hand of illusion
        Withdrew another fantasy in another direction.

        And the ocean of my endless days that gave no sign
    I was worthy of another life in another land. It now seems
More distant than the world I thought my demons had planned.

You brought me back to shore when I was bereft of either hope
    Or inspiration. And despite the uncertainty, I genuinely
        Believed you held a place for my redemption.

        Blessed by your enchanted ways I saw a glimmer
    A dilation in your eyes, imagined a place beyond
Reality where we would reach for the skies

You inspired a desire to lift me up from the waves with the
    Breath of attraction, but when the tide retreated I simply
        Realised you were a mirror of distraction.

43

Princess and Thorn

To flow easily in their eyes,
And dance with their demeanor,
Like goddesses upon high,
And enthroned in a classical arena.

What wonders one can achieve
With these blossoming flowers,
Princesses to be admired,
Imprisoned in their golden towers.

Potentials in time, their love
And affection encourages us to fall,
Inflaming powers of emotion,
Towards places that affect us all.

The realisation you failed the bud
You once cherished and chose,
Tentative with her love, and resilient
Until she became a prickly Rose.

She shines a light that casts
Shadows upon the path I made,
Reminding me, that even
The brightest candle will slowly fade.

Shadows of the Past

Imaginary places that flickered the industries of
My mind,
Magical forms, dimensions of myself I so wanted
To find.

I just needed to run out in time to know there was
A past,
Beyond seeds I had sown, towards stories I had yet
To cast.

To exist in a place beyond my world I would
Never see,
I embraced an illusion of someone else I thought I
Could be.

I wish I had lived a little more in those moments I can
Barely refer,
No more than secluded memories, reminiscing on how
They were.

And while I stand alone in this dream, my distant wish come true,
I see only loved ones left behind, the ghosts of people I
Once knew.

A Vision of the Future

I saw worlds in collision and fires in the sky -
Empty streets abandoned and towns left to die.
Fields we once relied on for the purpose of our grain -
Now consumed by oceans, their tides no longer contained.

I saw continents divided and cities layered in dust -
Intricate machines we once depended on now turned to rust.
Cards from which they were activated, our symbols of worth -
No longer of value, discarded and returned to earth.

I saw the sun shine with a reflection I hadn't previously seen -
Half as bright with fewer people than I remembered there had been.
And on the horizon a new moon cast a shadow in a strange light -
The old world had disappeared and the days turned into night.

The Covenant

And the Covenant has decreed, we stand in this place,
To feel and understand the grand design of his plan
With all wounds healed, and dreams revealed
We shall finally know if we have grown in time
As a mouse unto a lion, a man unto his soul
As a waning star unto the crystalized fountain
That seals the cross of eternal love and creation.

Subtle Connections

The ignorance of a lost world
That has touched the ocean

Of a far-away dream in which we once played,
Among the fluttering white buttercups

That avoided the eye, the memories of joy
We so easily forget. We are alone in this world.

As we are at peace with our destiny,
Yet we share in the tranquility of its final- outcome.

To leave as silently as we came,
With nothing more than the subtle connections

That remind us of who we are,
Where we are from, and where we are going.

Quarrel with Time

If I have wandered this path many times before,
Then it is true I have ridden the waves of every emotion -

I have lived and I have died, been bereft by uncertainty
But always with a sense of purpose and devotion.

If I have killed in the ages then I have been killed as a
Consequence.
If I have loved as I have loved, then my quarrel with time is no
More -

Beyond these restrictions and the veil of truth you have hidden,
It is only right you bring back to me the girl that I adore.

Shenley Park and the Voyage Home

A thousand days I have lay with this pain of emotion,

Their time and place were revealed, the eye of a tremendous storm
Where even the trickles of love would appear concealed.

And while the universe of my mind could not,

Set beyond the sky, I began to accept this is where it would finish,
The conclusion, it's purpose and the place I would die.

Then in a quiet moment, a shimmering light,

Took me unaware, a glance into her wondrous space that promised an
Illusionary world in which someone would care.

And in the joy of her accepting smile,

I finally set sail on my journey home, with love lost and love found,
It was the place I would forever roam.

The Light of Dawn

I have seen the darkest branches of the forest,
Left cold and disheartened. I imagined,
An existence beyond the perennial night
That saw no dawn. And now I find myself
At peace in this place. With the scatterings
Of my mind, I wonder what it might have been
If I had always felt like this.
Perhaps it has always been this way.
I only needed to see who I was inside
And be content with that knowledge,
As it would soon become my sanctuary.
It felt like they were shielding me
From the sunlight, when in fact they were
Protecting me from an element
Of my journey, I was afraid to embark.

The Dawn of Another Sun

It is good to know something
Has drawn to its exuberant end.
Balanced on the cusp of being,
A seedling breaking forth to the light.

A fleeting moment- a shooting star.
To reflect, to rejoice, to remember
The precious experiences that
Cradled you to the dawn of another sun

And in the symbols of life's innocent glories
Your achievements own vibrant skies
Bring forth all that flowers and sustains
A distant place, in mind subsides

Impetuous afflictions, the magic of days
Inquisitive perceptions, uneasy with time
Will rise in your reflection to remind you,
All that was, that is, and will forever be.

That Old Friend

It was strange when we met, so much had happened,
In the worlds I had travelled, that I barely recognized
The impish smile, the anticipation in his eyes,
And of the stories I would tell on my return.
That old friend, how could I forget you.

You had changed somewhat from when I remembered,
Although I had changed a lot more. How I wished
I could tell you of the wonders I had seen, the fairytales
Of my journeys into life's unknowns, of Gods and chariots
And the lands you used to dream.

I had seen many wonders, although there were so many
More to see. And the fairytales, although abundant
On my travels, I didn't always understand their purpose,
But the lands that rolled before me
Were much greater than you imagined.

I only returned to see you briefly, to let you know
I was okay. You dreamed a great story and I still carry the torch,
But the lands are far too tempting to turn back now.
You did well young friend, and you succeeded
In ways you could never have foreseen.

I came back to tell you there was a better dream,
Not too dissimilar but one much more fulfilling
That will take us to the next realm. You will know of me again
When you dream the next adventure. He will find me
And return a sign to you. We begin to make progress,

63

And it's starting to make sense.
As he began to fade, I looked back at his reflection,
And like a soft summer breeze that heralded the end of the season,
I could see the world around him slowly change,
And then my own because of it.

Goodbye old friend,
We will know each other again,
It's just a bigger world than you thought.

The Journey Home

Shadowless lines of amber
That emanate through the eternal night,
Of loves that were lost
And pains that were sown

And with each trickle of rain
That washes over our sorrow,
Encompassed and dimmed
By each returning light

Shepherded along by joyous angels
As witnesses to the truth,
We have lived, we have loved
And we have grown.

Golden Years

I mourn the passing of their
Years

Through photographs of
Innocents

Long since grown to
Strangers;

My cherubim's flown to let
Me

Grieve out golden days as if
They

Were a dream, as they all
Belonged

To another time and
Place,

Another mother; as if the
Years

Between had been but golden
Dreams.

Their impish grins I grieve,
I grieve.

Like a Hamlyn mother, I
Long

          To hear the returning piper
Bring

          Them home again once
More

          My playmates on an ageless
Green.

Val Leon
1940-2004

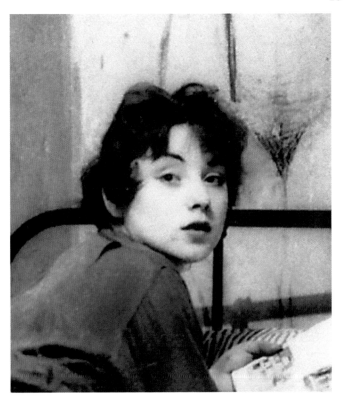

Note to readers:

Should ye find yourself
On a journey of mysticism
Tilt your head to the stars and moon above
Your ears to the wild lands below
And your nose to the wicked wind that surrounds ye

-Maisydel Fenn

Wisdom to the reader:

1. Look upon everyone as they are *now*, and not who they have been, or what they might become.
2. Shine the light within yourself as you would like to see it shine within others.
3. Know that there is no 'one love' and there is no 'one person' you can love. It goes everywhere or nowhere.
4. Speak the truth, even if it creates a space between those with whom you are bonded to. If they are worthy of your honesty, they will return.
5. Walk tentatively among the patterns of others, choose your words carefully and act with integrity.

A parting word to the reader:

Being in the Light of Love

The joy in life is love, and it is only with true love,
or the extension of that energy,
are we free to explore who we really are.

Without it we are always someone else.
If you do not feel love,
or you are unable to express it,

then it is impossible to be who you are meant to be,
and unlikely to achieve your potential.

We put great emphasis on what others think of us,
and yet that shouldn't even matter,
or does it matter what we think of them.

It is how we feel about them which will ultimately
determine how they feel about us.
However, like everything else in creation, it begins with yourself.

Only love has the power to change what we think
and not the other way around.

Index of First Lines

Way out in a distant realm
What did I do to change the way you looked into my eyes.
What is this intriguing flower that flutters and deflects
What is this magnetism that blew in from the trees.
When you dream upon a star.
We dance around the stars.

Index of Titles

That Old Friend
The Covenant
The Dawn of Another Sun
The Eyes of Three Fish

The Face in the Picture
The Journey Home
The Light of Dawn
The Roll of a Drum
The Solitude of Change

Unspoken Words

Visions in Time

Printed in Great Britain
by Amazon

33253861R00048